NO HUMAN WAY TO KILL

ROBERT PRISEMAN

SEABROOK PRESS

CONTENTS

This book is dedicated to the memory of Tony Seabrook
and supported by the Human Rights Centre, University of Essex

HUMAN RIGHTS CENTRE

Artwork: Robert Priseman

Design: Jovan Djordjevic

Research: Gail Aguilar Castañon, Robert Priseman

Text: Cathy Harrington, Robert Priseman,
                    Professor Sir Nigel Rodley, Anthony Ross
                    and Jim Willett

Special thanks are due to Professor John Packer, Director of the Human Rights Centre
at the University of Essex, for conceiving this book, Mike Goldmark for conceiving and
funding the series of twelve etchings which provide the artwork within this book and
Jan and Ian Wilkinson of the Goldmark Atelier for their care, guidance and professionalism
in producing the etchings.

I would also like to thank the following people most warmly for their help, support and
friendship. Without them this book would not have been possible.

Remy Allard , Piers Bannister, Simon Bell, Mark Callcutt, John Finlay, Jess Kenny,
Marian Maguire, Kim Manning Cooper, Kate Mardell, Jeremy Marshall, Saiko Matsumaru,
Caroline Morton, Mary Murphy, Jeremy O'Sullivan, Michael Peppiatt, Aurélie Plaçais,
Vanessa Potter, John and Barbara Priseman, John Paul Pryor, Michael Rodgers,
Paul Rumsey, Chiara Sangiorgio, Ally Seabrook, Mary Seabrook, Dan Twyman, Ginny Waters,
Sara Wilbourne, Shannon Williamson and Jessica Wood.

INTRODUCTION

INTRODUCTION
Robert Priseman

In the early 1990's, whilst working as a portrait painter, I received a commission to produce a painting of the Sheriff of London, Anthony Moss. He had an office in the Old Bailey, London's central criminal court, and during one of our meetings he took me to see the condemned cell beneath the courts. It is the only cell in the Old Bailey which has two doors, one for the prisoner to enter, and another which once led out to the scaffold. I had anticipated a sense of the walls screaming, but when we entered, I found there was no feeling at all. The walls consisted of plain white tiles, similar to the kind you would find in a bathroom. It was as if emotion had nowhere to stick.

The encounter stayed with me. In 2004 I embarked on a series of paintings of empty hospital interiors. I was drawn to the transitional state they represent, offering a place of caring for the human body while simultaneously removing any trace of the individual. These interiors are designed with a necessary matter of factness which overrides our own emotional concerns. They treat all bodies without hierarchy, yet represent a patriarchy within their very fabric. While I was working on these paintings, I saw the Nick Broomfield documentary on Aileen Wuornos, 'Life and Death of a Serial Killer', and found myself thinking about the similarities between medical institutions and execution facilities.

I was particularly struck by photographs of the lethal injection chamber at Huntsville in Texas, which seemed to me to possess a strange and haunting beauty. The gurney on which the condemned are placed reminded me of a modern form of crucifixion. Keen to explore this idea further through painting, I initially broadened the theme with a series of twelve line drawings which examined different methods of execution used around the modern world. I wanted them to act as a detached mirror, reflecting on the subject without judgment. With the help of the Goldmark Atelier these drawings were turned into a set of etchings which were first seen at the University of Essex. John Packer, Director of the Human Rights Centre at Essex, approached me with the idea of using them as the basis for a book; this is the result.

A MOTHER'S STORY

A MOTHER'S STORY
Cathy Harrington

"I cannot wipe away your tears…I can only teach you how to make them holy",
Anthony De Mello, *Affirmation*

My life changed forever the night I received the call that my beautiful daughter and her roommate had been brutally murdered on November 1, 2004. A shroud of darkness fell over me in heavy layers, suffocating me with fear and despair. It was inconceivable that the vibrant shining essence, that for twenty-six years had been Leslie Ann Mazzara, the light of my life, my flesh, my blood, my youngest child, could be gone, extinguished forever. Her beautiful and promising life was stolen in the night, in an act of terror, in a gruesome act of selfish anger and rage. I was thrust on a journey through hell seemingly without end, and began a mother's mission to make meaning out of the meaningless.

The next eleven months were an unspeakable nightmare as the police investigation following false assumptions that Leslie was the murderer's target failed to find the killer. I fumbled through each day in a broken-hearted daze, confused and unconvinced that anyone would want to hurt Leslie. When Eric Copple, a friend of her roommate, Adrienne, turned himself in after the police revealed that the killer smoked a rare blend of Camel cigarettes, we were all stunned. I hadn't realized that I had been holding my breath all that time and that every muscle in my body had been braced from that moment until I received this long-awaited call which came in the middle of the night. I gasped for air like a victim of a near-drowning accident. We had been held in trauma space for almost a year, while this man, this murderer, married Adrienne's best friend, and had gone about his life as if nothing had happened. Stunned by the news, I braced myself for the next steps of the journey.

The many months that followed were filled with speculation about Eric Copple and about whether the prosecution would seek the death penalty. The District Attorney assured us that it would be his decision ultimately and after they did a full review of the case and a psychological profile on Eric, they would ask the families for their views before making that decision. We were told to be patient, to wait.

Meanwhile the media rushed in to exploit and sensationalize our tragedy. The American entertainment industry has developed an unsavory taste for violence and vulgarity. When murder is turned into entertainment, the sacred gift of life is diminished and our minds and hearts become calcified, our humanity suffers.

I sought counsel with anyone who might help me preserve Leslie's dignity and save us from the potential pain and suffering of a lengthy and very public trial. Sister Helen Prejean generously offered to speak with me, and her words of wisdom nourished me with hope. Sister Helen told me heart-wrenching stories about mothers of murderers that opened my mind and my heart to compassion. She pierced my darkness when she said, "Jesus asks us to stretch, Cathy. There are two arms of the cross; one side is for the victims and their loved ones and the other side of the cross holds the same light of love and hope, for the murderer and his family." For the first time I felt a measure of compassion for Eric's mother, and I could feel my heart open, suddenly aware that it had been clenched tightly like a fist. Looking back I must have been thinking that a broken heart had to be bound tightly like a tourniquet.

There has been a gradual adjustment since then as my eyes have slowly adapted to the dark. My Universalist faith teaches that ultimately all will be reconciled with God and that everyone is saved, even murderers. When I think of Eric as a child wounded by abuse, I feel sadness, a too common history shared by those who grow up to commit violent acts against others. Remarkably, Jesus was capable of forgiving his murderers as he suffered on the cross. As a Unitarian Universalist Christian minister, I seek to follow the teachings and the example of Jesus, but forgiving the murderer of my daughter and for the loss of my never-to-be-born grandchildren – babies that my arms ache to hold – still seems inconceivable to me.

But, even in the worst that life has to offer I've discovered that grace is present. "Grace is everywhere", Georges Bernanos' country priest said on his death bed, borrowing his dying words from St. Therese of Liseaux. It must be true, because I found that when I reached towards the heavens from the hollow emptiness of my sorrow, I found grace. Grace was there waiting for me, quenching my sorrow, a trusted companion on the lonely journey.

Will, a homeless friend that I met along the way, gave me his grandmother's Benedictine cross to remind me of God's love when I told him about Leslie's murder. Moved by his compassion and selfless generosity, the theology of the cross took on new meaning for me, and at Sister Helen's suggestion, I developed a relationship with Mary as a peer. After all, her son was murdered, and Mary spent the rest of her life making meaning. I carried that cross in my pocket for over two years and often found my fingers tracing the lines of the two arms as if praying in Braille. My life became a living prayer; there are two arms to the cross. Jesus asks us to stretch....

"Have you ever heard of a pinhole camera?" retired astronomer, Dr. Ed Dennison asked when I mentioned to him that Sister Helen had poked a tiny hole in my darkness. He demonstrated it to me by covering the window in his laundry room with foil and poking a tiny hole in the foil. We huddled in the darkness and waited. Impatiently, I squirmed in the dark stuffy room as my eyes slowly adjusted. I thought five minutes was surely enough, but Ed told us that it takes a full thirty minutes for our eyes to adjust to the dark. After ten minutes, he held up a white paper to the beam of light coming in through the tiny hole and we were astounded to see the trees from outside outlined on the paper. Gradually, we could see the details of the leaves and as we waited they became more intricate and clear. I was amazed at how I was sure that I could see clearly in a few minutes and how much more clarity there was in fifteen, and even more in twenty and twenty-five minutes. The trees were upside down, and though I haven't found a metaphor to properly explain that phenomenon, I had no problem understanding the metaphor of the pinhole camera and my journey toward forgiveness, parting my sea of despair and hopelessness one step at a time. I may never arrive, but it is the goal of forgiveness that I have set my compass. I believe it is our true north as Jesus demonstrated on the cross, the destiny of human potential that some have called becoming fully human, and perhaps this is the kingdom of God that Jesus understood so clearly. Forgiveness is not a destination, it is a journey I have come to understand.

Which brings me to my understanding of the death penalty and what I believe to be the multi-layered hidden tragedy beneath the conviction that the death penalty is "just" punishment. I don't have time to build a case for the multitude of reasons that the death penalty is impractical economically, unjust, racist, and so on. I can best speak of my own experience and of the insights that I have gained over the past four and one half years of finding my way in the dark. I liken it to four and one half minutes in the pinhole camera experiment. I am just beginning to see. If we had been forced to endure a trial and remain defended and held in trauma, there would have been no beam of light to penetrate and relieve the oppressive darkness – nothing to illumine the path. The death penalty not only serves to keep us in a dark stagnating hope; it serves to compound the violence, and escalates the conflict, limiting our human potential to find our true north. I don't yet have a glimpse of what forgiving the murderer of my precious child would be like, but I know that if I don't walk towards that hope, I will be doomed to dwell in despair and pain forever. It is about choosing life, again and again, day after day.

The German poet, Rainer Maria Rilke suggests that we think of God as a direction. I hold that in my heart as I put one step in front of the other, and as I slowly move toward clarity, I begin to think about the possibility of meeting Eric Copple face to face; a stipulation written into the plea agreement for a facilitated victim/offender dialogue. If Sister Helen is right about the two arms of the cross, and I believe she is, then Eric can also find his way towards wholeness. But, it is Eric's responsibility to take fully into his heart the reality of what he has done and let the guilt tear and rip apart his heart from the inside out, as his senseless and violent act resulting in the murders of Leslie and Adrienne have done to all who loved them and whose lives they touched. It is only then that healing will be possible for Eric. I pray it will be so.

I would say that what might be the most insidious tragedy of the death penalty is that if we wilfully murder murderers, how can we ever hope to become fully human, to complete the journey? Honestly, I'm terrified of facing the murderer of my child one day, and I don't know if I will have the courage and the grace to ever forgive, but it is my hope and prayer. All I can do is keep on walking in that direction and leave the rest up to the grace that I have come to know and trust.

Cathy Harrington is a parish minister in the Unitarian Universalist faith. Her daughter Leslie Ann Mazzara was murdered on November 1, 2004 at her home in Napa, California. Cathy negotiated a life sentence for her daughter's murderer, who had potentially been facing the death penalty.

A LIFE ON DEATH ROW

ROUTINES
Anthony Ross

I wake up early in the morning. That's when all the noisemakers have fallen asleep. Guys who incessantly engage in pointless arguments and banal babble: "If a gorilla and a grizzly had a fight who would win?" Shit like that. They make quite a racket during the day and well into the night, shouting over each other at insane decibels as if that would leapfrog their train wreck of logic to the forefront of the bedlam. Chaos is their escapism. A way to muffle the real noise in their own heads. A way to avoid, if only temporarily, having to deal with the wretched reality of being on death row. It's their routine.

Two hours before dawn it's real quiet. I can think. Get some work done. I pace back and forth in my cell as an alternative to meditation. It's much more effective in setting the tone of my mental focus. I have a cup of coffee. I don't eat breakfast. I stopped years ago when I found part of a rat in my oatmeal. That screwed up my taste buds for a while. I wash my face, brush my teeth, rake my fingers over my hair. I stretch while listening to classical music then exercise for an hour: callisthenics, push-ups, shadow boxing, running in place, triceps on the toilet, and curls with a towel slid through the bars. Statistically speaking, California death row prisoners are more apt to die from poor health or a drug overdose than be executed. I think it's important to stay in shape. I'm manic about it. I don't miss a day.

After my exercise routine I take a birdbath in the sink if it isn't my day to walk to the shower, something we get to do three days a week. It's 6:30am when I look out the window across from my cell. I try to gauge the weather conditions. That's my barometer for whether or not I'll go to the yard – on rainy and cold days I stay in. San Quentin prison sits on a peninsula overlooking the San Francisco Bay. During the winter months the prison can get covered in fog. We're put on lock down. No one gets to go out in the fog.

The windows are behind the gunrail. A guard, cradling a mini-14 assault rifle and wearing a holstered 38 revolver on his side like a cowboy, watches the tiers. He rarely sits down. He rarely looks out the window. He eats standing up. For eight hours he walks the entire length of the gunrail, about a quarter mile, back and forth. If the alarm goes off he runs up and down the gunrail looking for the trouble. He doesn't have to give a warning shot. He could kill without saying a word. That's his routine.

Any time I leave my cell I am searched. Anything I take with me is searched. A guard will examine every piece of clothing, every sheet of paper, and every cavity of my body. I have learnt to disassociate myself from the procedure. I stare straight ahead, right through him, as I lift up my scrotum. I am numb when I spread my cheeks and cough. I don't feel anything. Not anger. Not frustration. Not humiliation. There is a cold primal exactitude coursing through my veins, like a predator waiting for one precious moment. There are days when the cells are searched. What meagre possessions I own get tossed about and ramshackled. I don't take it personal. Afterwards I methodically return everything to its place. It doesn't matter how long it takes me. I do it. This is prison. This is the routine.

Alone. That's how I processed the news of over a dozen people dying in my family. It is the only emotional arch that can stir up feelings of vulnerability. Each loss makes me acutely aware of my isolation – 24 years. Each death gave me a precise sense of my own physical impermanence. I live with an intense sense of immediacy. I engage every day like a man on fire. From a single visit I can absorb a lifetime. In a single letter I could, in vivid detail, translate all the passion of an imprisoned man's heart. I have become stoic. Knowing any time I call home there could be another death. There was. My only blood brother died in a foreign country where he didn't even speak the language. He was alone. With his thoughts. His ghost. His regrets. I have watched my hair turn gray. Watched my youth dissolve with the pendulum-like swing of each day. Fear does not keep me company. I am ready to meet my fate. Birth. Decay. Death. This is life's routine.

State level appeal. Denied. Death sentence upheld. Incompetent attorneys. Same old story. For 24 years I have moved through the judicial maze like digested food slowly making its way to the final solution. I was the 107th person to join the exclusive group referred to as 'Dead Men'. I may leave them soon. As the number climbs towards 700, each face brings with it a reflection of what is wrong with the system. Each face is wrought with an impression of what is wrong in society. But what I am most struck by, is the sharp contrast between race, class, who gets death, and how it is also accepted as routine.

I have long ago come to terms with the possibility of dying here. I'm not overly philosophical about it. If it happens, I will have the luxury of knowing exactly when, where, and how I will die. No surprises. This insight has had an effect on me. But my self-transformation is of my own making. I have not had a personal experience with any god. My transcendental experience came the moment I realized that the last routine of my life may occur in this sequence:

Four guards in black fatigues will escort me from the death cell to the chamber. A spiritual advisor, if I want one, can accompany me. Once I'm in what used to be the gas chamber the guards strap me onto a gurney. The executioner locates a vein and sticks in an IV. When he's finished he'll look at the Warden for a signal at which point the Warden will ask me if I have any last words. Since I'm not big on monologue I'll shake my head no. The Warden then nods to the executioner who releases 5 grams of sodium pentathol via a 60cc syringe into my bloodstream. In no more than 60 seconds this knocks me out cold. The IV is then flushed with saline and 50cc of pancuronium bromide is sent through the line. This drug will paralyze every single muscle in my body except for the heart. My breathing slows as the muscles controlling the rib cage and diaphragm began to freeze up. The IV is again flushed with saline and the final poisonous chemical, 50cc of potassium chloride, is pumped into my body. This blocks the electrical impulses to the heart, stopping it from beating. The results – my lungs are imploding, my organs are writhing, and my brain is gasping for oxygen. The outward appearance will look uneventful, but internally, all hell is breaking loose. Death comes in less than 15 minutes. There will be nothing peaceful about it. The Warden will announce the time of my demise. But I tell you now, don't dare accept the claim that my murder was routine.

Anthony Ross (C-58000) is on death row in San Quentin State Prison, San Quentin, California, USA. A former member of the Crips Street Gang, he won the 1996 PEN Prison Writing Award for best short fiction.

THE DAY OF AN EXECUTION

THE DAY OF AN EXECUTION
Jim Willett

I will describe what a typical execution day consisted of for me when I was the Warden of the Huntsville "Walls" Unit, where all of the State's executions have taken place. The scene described is of an inmate who was fully cooperative, which approximately 86 of the 89 that I presided over were.

The reality of it being an execution day sometimes came to me as soon as I awoke. At other times it was with my first cup of coffee.

My morning began much like any other day for the Warden, fielding phone calls, visiting with employees and inmates, and answering correspondence, until nine o'clock. At that time I made a phone call to the Attorney General's Office in Austin. The purpose of this call was to talk with the attorney who was assigned this case. He would give me an update on how the case was going in the courts. It was rare not to have something working in the courts – the condemned inmate's attorney making every effort to stop the execution on various grounds. Once I got off the phone with the attorney, I'd call my supervisors and relay the information I'd just learned on to them. There were several other people that I'd call, those who'd be helping with the execution that night but who did not work on the Walls Unit with me. Some of these people were not regular employees of the prison system. The Huntsville Funeral Home was also appraised of where things were in the process.

Following these calls the day generally returned to normal. By now the Warden's secretary had brought several folders with certain bits of information for myself and some others. Another folder from the Public Information Office from across the street at the Old Administration Building would arrive also. It was basically the information that was being made available to the media. But the little manila folder held my interest more. It told me who was planning to attend the execution, including the inmate's invited guests, the victim's family members, and the media people who would attend the execution. Also, in this folder was the condemned man's last meal request. This seemed to be of interest to a lot of folks on the outside, although something the Walls Unit kitchen captain and the inmate cook had known for a couple of weeks. But this was the first time I'd laid eyes on the request. There was a picture of the condemned man also, but sometimes the fellow wound up not looking much like the photo. He'd aged a lot in a short period of time or maybe hadn't exercised much and the prison food had added pounds to his frame.

Throughout the morning there was the usual. Telephone calls coming in about routine goings on of the unit. Papers to sign. Written requests from inmates. Usually I'd have lunch in the Officers Dining Hall around eleven, something I did most every day. Afterwards was more of the normal routine until early afternoon.

The inmate arrives at the Death House and his (or her) restraints are removed once inside and the door to the building is secured. The inmate is strip-searched and then finger printed. Next he is placed in a cell and given a fresh set of clothes.

Most of them wanted to clean the ink from their hands and then I'd talk with the inmate to tell them what to expect for the afternoon and to also find out the mood of the inmate. Sometimes these conversations were short and to the point and at other times I might have to cut the inmate short and tell him I'd see him later. It was all dependent on the inmate and his willingness to talk. If it was obvious that the inmate did not care to have a long conversation then I went with the basics and left him for the chaplain to deal with. At the least I told him when and what to expect for the remainder of the day. I always asked if he expected to have any visitors, which at this point was down to a spiritual advisor and/or an attorney. I was lenient with phone calls and found out if the inmate wanted to make any phone calls. Often they wanted to call family and talk one last time. Sometimes they had a relative that had not been able to make the trip to visit at Death Row during the last visiting period. Sometimes these family members, and we had one mother, were locked up in the penitentiary. One brother was even in another state. This all calls for some coordination between the prisons. I always tried to find out from the inmate about the last statement. Did he plan to make one? If so, I warned him not to go over five minutes or so, or that I'd tell him to wrap it up. Also, I wanted him to tell me how I'd know when he was through. The reason for this was so I'd not cut him off before he was through with his last statement. And one thing I did that was outside the rules, I found out if they'd like a cigarette to smoke. Some rather strange conversations took place back there. Others had hardly a thing to say.

For the remainder of the afternoon the inmate will be in the presence of the prison chaplain and two security supervisors. Throughout the afternoon there will be other people who come and go to the cell block. The major and captain of the shift will likely drop in several times just to make sure everything is going smoothly.

The inmate is allowed only two types of visits while at the Walls Unit. One from a spiritual advisor and one from his attorney. The visits begin at 3 p.m. and last for thirty minutes each. During this time the inmate will be moved to #1 Cell which is the visiting cell. It is covered with a heavy black mesh wire to stop any contraband from being passed to the inmate. Once the inmate is secured in the cell, the visitor is escorted to the Death House and allowed to sit in a chair in front of the cell. During this visitation time the chaplain will go about two blocks north of the Walls to the Hospitality House where the inmate's family will be waiting. At this time he will tell them what to expect as they witness the execution.

At about 4:30 p.m. the inmate is given his last meal. The most requested last meal since lethal injections began in 1982 has been a cheeseburger and french fries. Some of the inmates eat a hearty meal only a couple of hours before the scheduled execution.

At about five minutes before six o'clock I'd put my coat on and tell everyone in the warden's offices that it was time to head to the back (to the Death House). Myself, along with whatever supervisors of mine that were present would go to the room where the executioner was and await the phone calls. At six o'clock an official who ranks above the warden will receive two phone calls from Austin. The phone calls will be taken in what is known as the IV Room, next to the Death Chamber. One phone call is from the Attorney General's Office and the other from the Governor's Office. They will tell the official that we may proceed with the execution. At this point I would cross the Death Chamber and enter into the Death Row cell block. I would walk up to the front of the cell where the inmate was waiting. I called him by his last name and told him that it was time to come with me to the next room, meaning the Death Chamber. One of the officers would then unlock the locks to the cell and open the door. I would tell the inmate to follow me to the next room. The tie-down team would have joined the other Death House officers shortly before six o'clock. These officers along with the chaplain would escort the inmate, unrestrained, usually, and without placing a hand on him, into the Death Chamber. Once the inmate is in the Death Chamber he is told, usually by me, to get onto the gurney and lie down with his head on the pillow. The straps to the gurney are all undone. The officers quickly strap the inmate with all of the straps (one around each ankle and arm and others over the body). When they were done with the straps I physically checked each one and asked the inmate if any were too tight. On two or three occasions the inmate stated that a certain one was tight and one of the officers loosened it a notch. I then dismissed the officers back into the cell block.

At this point I walked over and opened the door to the IV Room. The medical team would enter the room and in a matter of minutes would have the inmate hooked up with an IV in each arm. While they worked, I would talk to the inmate, if he wanted to talk. I stood opposite the medical team. They always began with the inmate's right arm. Tubes run from the arms through a small window on the wall of the IV Room where the drugs have been mixed a short time earlier and sit on a table in the room. The medical team returns to the IV Room. The inmate is now completely hooked up on the gurney with only the chaplain and me in the room with him. During the time the medical team was hooking up the IVs, a mike has been lowered to just above his head. The amplifier is hooked to speakers that are in the other rooms of the Death House. Another line feeds a speaker that is in the Warden's Office. The Warden's secretary would record the inmate's last statement for the press. She also keeps a record of what is going on and when. A person on the phone watching through a slightly opened crack in the cell block door will relay this information to her.

For a few short moments it is just the three of us in that little room, the chaplain, myself, and the inmate strapped to the gurney. The chaplain and I are usually close to the inmate's head at this time but we will back away as the witnesses begin entering the witness rooms. I will be nearest the inmate's head and the chaplain beside his feet. Soon the victim's witnesses are brought into the West witness room. They are escorted by Victims' Services staff and usually the Major of the Walls Unit. Five witnesses are allowed unless there are multiple victims and then a sixth person is allowed. Once they are in the room other members of the staff will escort the inmate's witnesses to the East witness room. The inmate can invite five witnesses but can have a sixth if he wishes to invite his spiritual advisor. There are also five members of the news media allowed and they are scattered in both rooms. The Huntsville Item newspaper, the Huntsville radio station, a member of the Associated Press, and two others, usually from the area of the crime scene, are the normal makeup. There is also a captain in the East room along with a Texas Ranger. Our own Public Relations Office will have at least one person in a witness room. Once the witnesses are in place, I would tell the inmate that he may make a last statement. Most of them made a statement. Most lasted three minutes or less. When the inmate completed his statement I would give a signal to the executioner to begin the execution process. The executioner is, of course, in the IV Room behind a one-way glass window. He can see through to the Chamber but no one can see into the IV Room through the glass.

About 30 seconds after I gave the signal, the inmate would take his last breath. About two and a half minutes from the time of the signal, the executioner would signal me that all the drugs have been put into the inmate. I waited three minutes before bringing in the doctor. The reason I did this is simply that the Warden before me advised me to wait to make sure all the fluids had taken effect. It worked for me the first time and I chose not to mess with changing something that worked. I can tell you that the first time was the longest three minutes of my life. I would then get the doctor who is waiting in the cell block. The doctor would examine the inmate, doing all those things that doctors do to make sure a body is dead, checking for pulse, checking the eyes with a small flashlight, etc., and then he would pronounce the inmate dead, giving a time of death in doing so. The doctor then goes through the door back into the cell block. The process, from the time of the two phone calls until the doctor pronounces death, usually took in the neighborhood of 25 minutes.

The witnesses were taken from the witness rooms one group at a time beginning with the victim's witnesses. Once the rooms were cleared the medical team would remove the medical devices and retreat back into the IV Room. The officers would then remove the leather straps. The funeral home immediately came in and took the body.

The legal papers are then signed in the Warden's secretary's office by the doctor and the top ranking official. Everyone then goes home.

AN INTERVIEW WITH
WARDEN JIM WILLETT

AN INTERVIEW WITH WARDEN JIM WILLETT
Robert Priseman

Robert Priseman: What are the ideal personal qualities required for someone who is going to be on an execution team?

Jim Willett: Someone of good character, who is conscientious about his work quality and who can work with others. This person needs to be understanding of the inmate's situation and be able to adapt to any actions/non-actions by the inmate. This person must be in control of their emotions and remain dedicated to their job assignment.

RP: What is the most difficult part of an executioner's job?

JW: I have never been the executioner and cannot answer this question. I will respond from the only perspective I know, and that is of the Warden, the one who oversees the executions. Not to be short, and I am not trying to oversimplify this matter, but for me watching a person die and knowing that I have given the signal to cause the death is the most difficult part of the execution process.

RP: Have you ever witnessed a botched execution? If so, what feelings came to the fore for you?

JW: My idea of a botched execution is one in which the drugs were administered and the person is not dead. I have never witnessed this. I have seen times when veins were hard for the medical people to find and some of these times when a vein was used that was in a place other than the arm or hand, which was usually used.

RP: What level of training is necessary for a medic on the execution team?

JW: Someone with a medical background in starting IVs and in high pressure situations is ideal. I used to think that someone who had been a medic in the Vietnam War was a good candidate.

RP: Did you ever think about leaving your role on executions?

JW: I never thought about leaving my job as the Warden at the Death Chamber, except when I was ready to retire. As much as I did not like working the executions, I knew it was my job until I retired.

RP: Did you find that you needed to distance yourself emotionally from what you were doing, and if so, how did you manage that?

JW: Once I had taken part in several executions and had the routine of the process, at least my part, down, it became easier to deal with. Not easy. At that time my job became more of overseeing the operation and being available to everyone, including the inmate. I am somewhat of an emotional person, so I worked at keeping my mind on the job and making sure that everything went as smoothly as possible.

RP: Do you think facing the death penalty forces the condemned to face up to their crime in a way that an ordinary prison sentence doesn't?

JW: I think that an inmate who is facing the death penalty is probably more aware of his losses than a person doing some other sentence. Surely the finality is greater and thus the whole incident which caused it is more magnified than that of non Death Row inmates. Many who arrive at the Death House for their last few hours have become Christians and many of these view looming death with an obvious spiritual strength.

RP: What is the average length of time a prisoner spends on Death Row?

JW: The last time I researched this, about a year or so ago, it was down to nine and a half years. If I recall correctly, when I arrived back at the Walls Unit, the average time was twelve years. Most of this probably has to do with a change in the laws concerning the appeals process and how it is handled.

RP: Some inmates on Death Row have requested their own execution date, why is that?

JW: My guess is that they are tired of waiting in their cells, with nothing much to do. Prior to the escape in 1998 at the Ellis Unit, many were allowed to work and recreation was similar to what the general prison population had. However, with the move to the (then Terrell) Polunsky Unit, they do not work and basically spend the day in their cells. Not much of a way to do time.

RP: Do you think executions provide 'closure' for the victims' families?

JW: I had little contact with the families of the victims. My observations of them were from a distance but I did have the feeling that they may not have received the closure that they might have expected.

RP: How do you view the media's role in the execution process?

JW: I think the media's role in the execution process is to report the facts as witnessed about the execution. To me, the set up in Texas works just fine. The media here are allowed to come with the other witnesses shortly after the condemned is readied for execution.

RP: Do you think the media report on all executions equally?

JW: Typically, the media from the area where the murder occurred will cover the execution, pretty much equal all the time. The larger media, the national media, will report on an execution if they think their audience wants to hear about it. Or, if prominent people are concerned with it, or if an agenda is being pushed. I think the bottom line is, will it make their ratings better.

RP: Why do you think most condemned don't struggle on their final journey?

JW: Most of the men who I watched die on the gurney did not struggle when it came time to move them from the Death House holding cell to the Execution Chamber. Nor did they struggle on the gurney when the officers buckled the many straps over their bodies. I would guess that these men have for the most part accepted their fate. Some of them were quite calm and many of them had become Christians and seemed ready to step into eternity.

RP: Do you ever find yourself thinking about any of the prisoners you have taken the final walk with?

JW: I actually never think about the executions or these men/woman except when I am asked about it as part of my job at the Texas Prison Museum or with media people.

RP: Having seen such a large number of people in the position of being a condemned prisoner, do you feel there is a 'typical' pattern that leads a person down this path?

JW: Robert, I don't know that I ever noticed a pattern with these folks, although I was never looking for one either. Thinking back about them, I recall each one as totally different from the rest, but my interest in them was not about how they got there. That just didn't play much of part of my job. I do recall about some, thinking while conversing with them, that... how did this man get so screwed up as to be here in front of me in this situation?

RP: Has your role as Warden made you view life differently to how you saw it before?

JW: You know, I look at it like this, that I saw death in a way that very few people do. I saw people's lives taken because they took someone else's life. I saw people die who knew beforehand the day of their death. I saw people who had the opportunity to say "I'm sorry" to people, or to say, "I love you" in earnest because they knew that it was their last opportunity. I watched people die who were perfectly healthy. And, I watched these people die at a moment shortly after I gave a signal to end their life. I think the view of life that is different, or at least more thoughtful than before seeing these deaths, is just how messed up things can get when one doesn't follow God's laws. So many people wind up with a lifetime of hurt. It made me realize how important it is to love God and to love your neighbor. And to obey His law.

This interview took place on the 24th February 2009

Jim Willett was Warden of the Huntsville 'Walls' Unit in Texas where he oversaw the execution by lethal injection of 89 prisoners. In 2000 he won a Peabody Award for his account of deathrow, 'Witness to an Execution'.

33

TWELVE METHODS OF EXECUTION

ELECTRIC CHAIR

'Electric Chair' shows the de-commissioned chair of West Virginia State Penitentiary at Moundsville, USA and is based on a photograph taken by Beth Santore. Electrodes are placed on the body of the condemned and between 500 and 2,000 volts are passed through it for around thirty seconds. After a pause, a second jolt is applied resulting in the death of the prisoner by electrocution.

Ink on paper, 30.5cm x 30.5cm, 2007

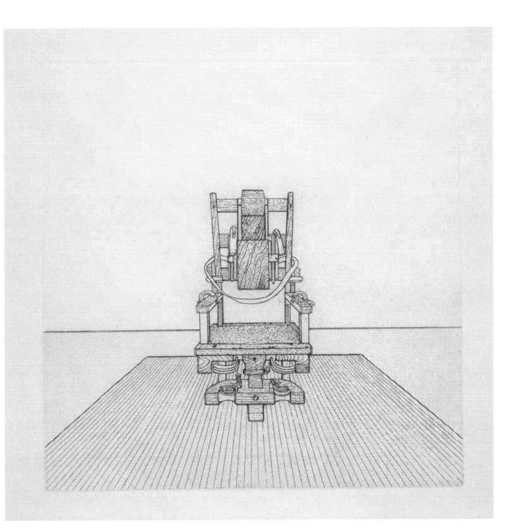

EXECUTION CHAMBER

This etching depicts the Execution Chamber of San Quentin State Prison, California, USA. Originally designed as a gas chamber it was adapted for use as a lethal injection facility after 1992. The etching is based on a photograph supplied courtesy of the California Department of Corrections and Rehabilitation.

Ink on paper, 30.5cm x 30.5cm, 2007

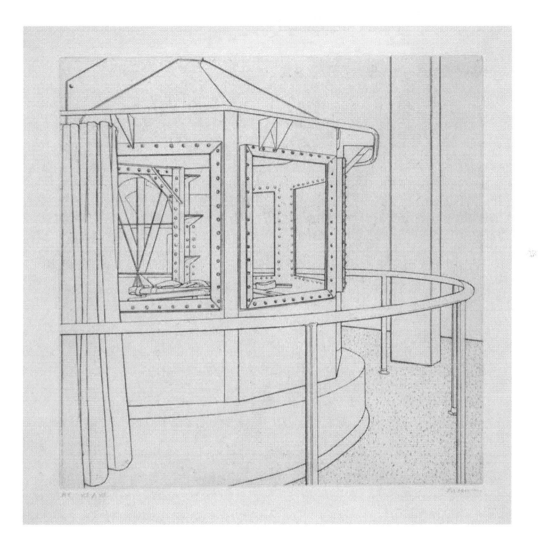

FIRING SQUAD RESTRAINT CHAIR

The 'Firing Squad Restraint Chair' depicts the execution method used in Utah State Prison, Draper, USA. It is based on an Associated Press Photograph, supplied courtesy of PA Photos. The chair sits on a pan designed to collect bodily fluids and is surrounded by polythene sheeting. The condemned person is hooded and shot in the heart by a team of five marksmen.

Ink on paper, 30.5cm x 30.5cm, 2007

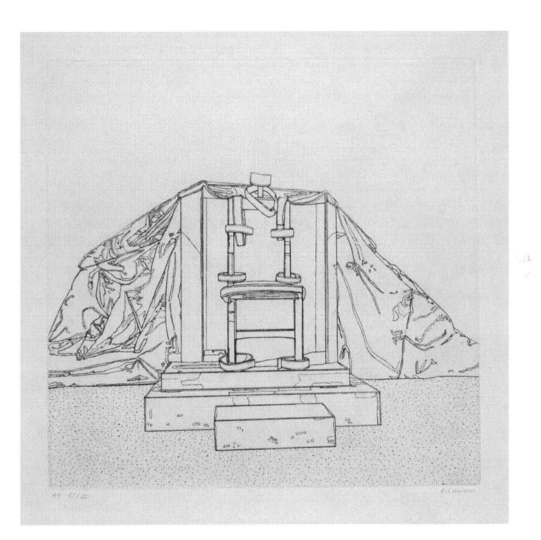

41

FIRING SQUAD WALL

The etching shows the courtyard of the stone breakers' yard in Kilmainham Gaol, Dublin, Ireland. Condemned prisoners stood blindfold in front of the wall, hands tied behind their back, with a piece of white paper pinned over their heart. Execution was carried out by a firing squad of twelve men.

Ink on paper, 30.5cm x 30.5cm, 2007

GARROTTE

This etching is composed of an amalgamation of three images and shows a wooden seat on which the prisoner is seated. A metal collar is placed around the neck, then a spike with a screw thread at the back of the garrotte is turned in order to sever the spinal cord. The garrotte was last used in Spain on March 2, 1974.

Ink on paper, 30.5cm x 30.5cm, 2007

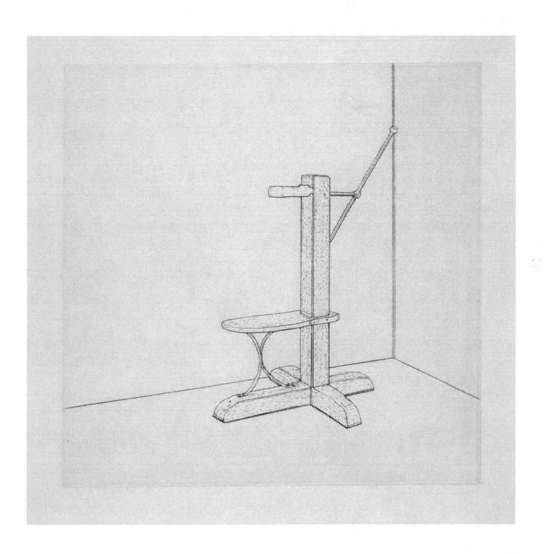

GAS CHAMBER   (Auschwitz)

The gas chambers at Auschwitz Concentration Camp, Poland had pellets of Zyklon B dropped into them through a vent in the ceiling. Zyklon B was originally used as a rat poison and is a form of hydrogen cyanide which causes death through hypoxia. Early examples of Nazi gas chambers held twenty-five people at a time while later chambers were designed to hold up to 2,500 people and were in use until 1945.

Ink on paper, 30.5cm x 30.5cm, 2007

GAS CHAMBER (Colorado)

This image shows the Colorado gas chamber, Colorado, USA and is derived from a photograph taken by Richard Nowitz. Potassium cyanide pellets are dropped into a pail containing sulphuric acid which is located under the chair where the prisoner is restrained. The resulting chemical reaction generates hydrogen cyanide gas resulting in death by hypoxia.

Ink on paper, 30.5cm x 30.5cm, 2007

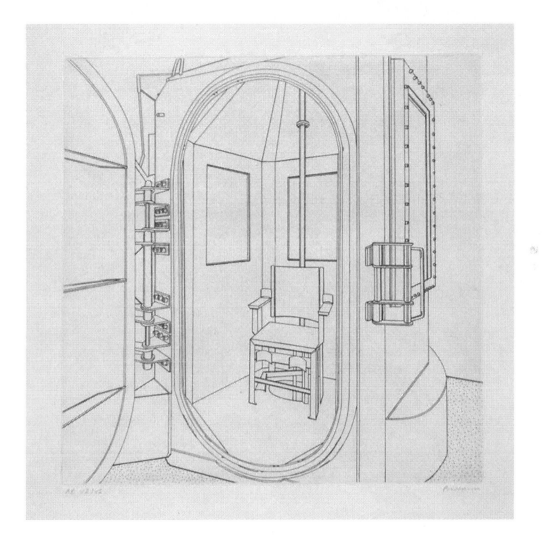

49

GUILLOTINE

The guillotine was first used in France in 1791. This etching is based on a photograph taken in Tunisia around 1900, and shows a Berger Machine. Death results from decapitation, with the severed head remaining conscious for between thirteen to thirty seconds. The guillotine was last used on September 10, 1977, at Baumettes Prison in Marseilles.

Ink on paper, 30.5cm x 30.5cm, 2007

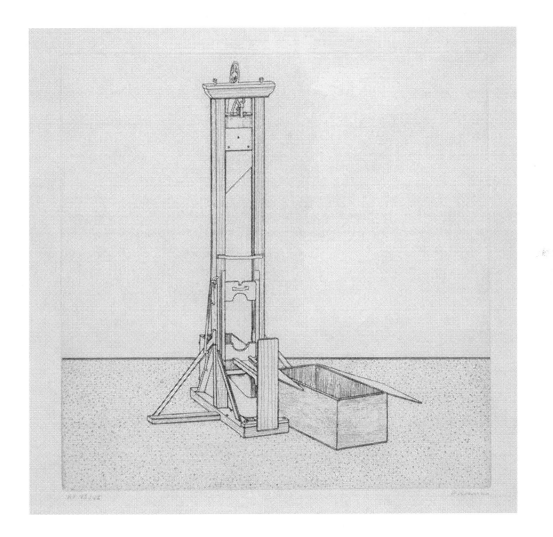

LETHAL INJECTION

'Lethal Injection' shows the gurney at Texas State Penitentiary, Huntsville, Texas, USA. It is derived from a number of images with the primary source of reference being a photograph supplied courtesy of Alan Pogue. Execution by this method involves injecting the inmate with a series of drugs which are designed to induce rapid unconsciousness followed by paralysis of the respiratory system and cessation of the heart beat.

Ink on paper, 30.5cm x 30.5cm, 2007

53

STONING

Stoning is an ancient form of execution which is mentioned in the Bible. The Islamic Penal Code of Iran prescribes it as a punishment for offences which include adultery. When carried out, convicted men are buried up to the waist and convicted women up to the chest. Palm sized stones are then thrown at the prisoner by an assembled group until the prisoner dies or escapes.

Ink on paper, 30.5cm x 30.5cm, 2007

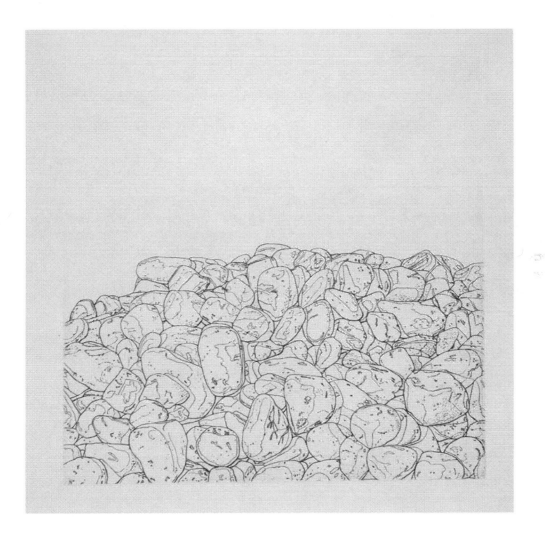

TRAP DOOR GALLOWS

The 'Trap Door Gallows' shows the former execution cell at Wandsworth Prison in London, England. It is based on a photograph taken around 1900. The method uses gravity as the force to break the neck of the prisoner, taking into account their age, height and weight. The last hangings in England took place on August 13, 1964.

Ink on paper, 30.5cm x 30.5cm, 2007

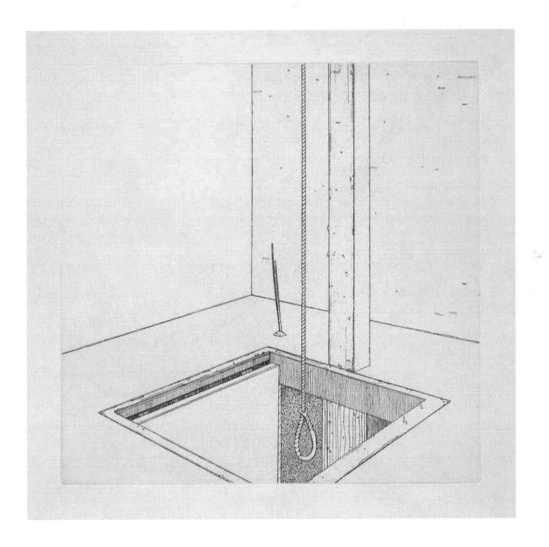

TRUCK CRANE

The truck crane is a method used for public hanging in Iran. A noose is placed around the neck of the condemned and attached to the grab hook of the crane, of which the arm is then extended. The condemned is raised by the neck, resulting in death by strangulation; with brain death taking three to five minutes and body death five to fifteen minutes.

Ink on paper, 30.5cm x 30.5cm, 2007

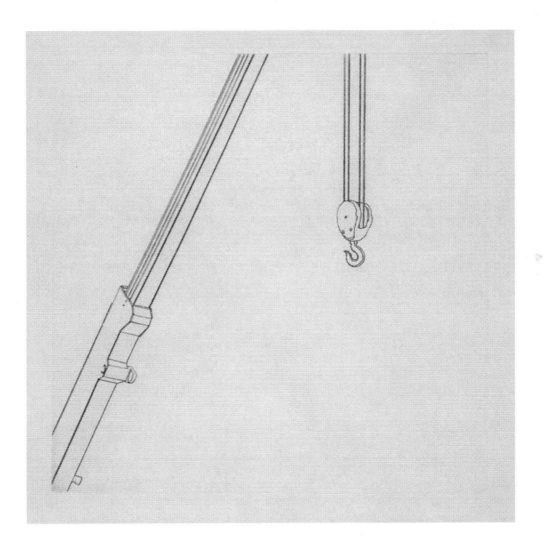

FACTS

ELECTRIC CHAIR

The Electric Chair is a method of execution used only in the USA. It was developed in response to a call made by the New York State legislature in 1886 to find a more humane alternative to executing prisoners than by hanging.

Thomas Edison, the US inventor and businessman who had established himself in the electrical utility industry in 1882 with a DC service, conducted a number of experiments in 1887 which involved electrocuting animals lured onto a metal plate which had been wired to a 1,000 volt AC generator. The AC current was developed in 1886 by George Westinghouse and reverses direction in a circuit at regular intervals whereas the DC current flows in one direction only.

In 1888, the inventor Harold P. Brown went to Edison's New Jersey laboratory to carry out research. He subsequently developed the first electric chair which utilized Westinghouse's AC current rather than the DC current sold by Edison. The first Electrical Execution Act went into effect in the United States on January 1, 1889. William Kemmler, a prisoner in Auburn Prison, New York, became the first person to be electrocuted. The execution took place on August 6, 1890. It took two attempts to kill Kemmler, which lasted for a period of eight minutes. During the execution, Kemmler's blood vessels ruptured causing bleeding and his body caught fire.

During an electrocution, a conductive sponge is placed on the shaven head of the prisoner. Electrodes are then attached to the head and ankles of the condemned and between 500 and 2,000 volts are passed through the body for a period of around thirty seconds. The current surges and is then turned off. Doctors wait for the body to cool down before examining it for a heartbeat. If the prisoner's heart is still beating, a second jolt is applied. Post-mortem is delayed after an electrocution to give the internal organs time to cool.

The Electric Chair is available as a method of execution in Alabama, Arkansas, Florida, Illinois, Oklahoma, South Carolina, Kentucky, Tennessee and Virginia. The last person executed by electric chair was James Earl Reed on June 20, 2008 in South Carolina.

FIRING SQUAD

A firing squad is traditionally formed to execute military prisoners who face the death penalty as a result of court martial for crimes such as cowardice, desertion and mutiny. It is typically made up of between three to six marksmen who are sometimes known as 'peace officers'. The firing squad will usually stand at a distance of around twenty feet in front of the condemned. The condemned in turn will be tied to a chair or stake and be blindfolded. Then, a white cloth will be pinned to their chest, which will act as a target. It is typical for one anonymous member of the firing squad to be issued with a blank cartridge, enabling each marksman to remain uncertain as to who fired the fatal shot. Members of the squad, aiming at the condemned's chest, are required to shoot simultaneously on the command to fire. Bullets fired at the chest rupture the heart, large blood vessels and lungs, causing the prisoner to die of haemorrhage and shock.

If the initial attempt to end the prisoner's life fails, the officer in charge will fire a 'coup de grâce' shot to the head to end the condemned's life.

Death by firing squad remains a permitted form of execution in Idaho, Oklahoma and Utah, where the procedure requires the prisoner to be seated on a chair. The prisoner's body is then restrained by straps to the head, limbs and waist with a white Velcro patch placed over the area of the heart. The chair, placed on a platform, is surrounded by sandbags or black plastic sheeting to capture blood splatter. A black hood is then pulled over the inmate's head.

On January 17, 1977 at Utah State Prison in Draper, the execution by firing squad of Gary Gilmore marked a return to the death penalty in the USA after a previous US Supreme Court suspension of executions in 1967. He was shot by a team of five men with .30 calibre rifles loaded with single rounds.

The last execution by firing squad in the USA was carried out in Utah on January 26, 1996 on John Albert Taylor. Taylor elected to die by firing squad rather than lethal injection, which was an alternative available to him.

THE GARROTTE

The garrotte was initially used as a method of torture. The original use of the word 'garrotte' applied to strangulation by any implement. It was introduced in Spain as the single civilian method of execution at the beginning of the reign of Ferdinand VII. A similar device had also been used in China which was known as the bowstring. With the bowstring, the condemned stood, tied, with their back to an upright post. In the post two holes were bored, through which the cord of a long bow was passed. The cord was placed around the neck of a condemned prisoner and pulled tightly until they died of strangulation.

The Spanish garrotte was similar to the Chinese bowstring. However, the Spanish garrotte seated the condemned on a low shelf in front of a shorter post. Two pieces of metal in the shape of a collar which were attached to the post were secured around the neck of the prisoner. Strapped at the legs, arms and waist, a lever connected to the collar through the post was turned by the executioner. This tightened the collar until the prisoner died of strangulation.

An alternative version known as the 'Catalan garrotte' incorporated a spike into the end of the lever. This passed through back of the collar and pierced the condemned's neck in order to break it between the second and third vertebrae. This was performed in an attempt to ensure the prisoner did not strangle to death. The executioner typically turned the lever three times before death occurred.

The garrotte was last used in Spain on March 2, 1974, when Heinz Chez in Tarragona and Salvador Puig Antich in Barcelona were simultaneously executed after having been condemned in separate incidents for killing police officers. The last female garrotting was on a twenty-eight year old woman on May 19, 1959. The Garrotte was also used in the Spanish colonies of Cuba, Mexico, Puerto Rico and The Philippines as well as in Portugal.

The last executions to be carried out in Spain were on September 27, 1975 when two members of ETA and three members of FRAP were shot by firing squad. Use of the death penalty in Spain came to an end following the death of General Franco.

GAS CHAMBER (Auschwitz)

The Nazi gas chambers located at Auschwitz concentration camp, Poland, used pellets of Zyklon B which were dropped into them through a vent in the ceiling. Zyklon B is a crystal form of cyanide originally designed as a rat poison.

The first use of a gas chamber by the Nazis during the Second World War was at Fort VII, Poznan, in Poland. A nearby hospital at Owinska which treated mentally ill patients was requisitioned by the German Army in mid-September 1939, with the aim of converting it into a barracks for the SS. The Nazi commissioner appointed to be in charge of Owinska mental hospital requested that a list of all its patients be drawn up. The staff of the hospital were informed that the patients were to be moved to alternative hospitals. In the second half of October the first batch of patients was then collected for reassignment under the surveillance of the SS. Trucks left the hospital every day and drove to Fort VII. Each truck held about twenty-five patients. Once there, the patients were unloaded from the truck and placed into an adapted bunker within the courtyard. The doors of the bunker were closed behind them and sealed off with clay. Gas was then pumped into the bunker until all the patients had died.

A group of specially assigned prisoners at Fort VII were instructed to remove the corpses from the bunker which were then loaded onto trucks and driven away. Many of the inmates at Fort VII were later transferred and the SS Commandant in charge became the first Commandant of Chelmno Extermination Camp.

Gas chambers in Nazi occupied Europe developed in scale to the point where prisoners were loaded onto trains which went directly to extermination and concentration camps such as the one at Auschwitz. Once there, prisoners could be unloaded and taken directly to gas chambers capable of holding and executing 2,500 people at one time.

Zyklon B is still manufactured for use as a rat poison in the Czech Republic under the trade name Uragan D2.

GAS CHAMBER   (single person use)

The gas chamber was developed in Nevada, USA in 1923 to kill twenty-nine year old prisoner Gee Jon. Prison authorities initially tried to kill Jon by pumping cyanide gas into his cell. This attempt failed when the gas leaked and led to the development of an airtight chamber which was first used in Nevada on February 8, 1924 to kill Jon.

The gas chamber kills the prisoner when crystals of sodium cyanide are dropped into a pail of sulphuric acid which is located underneath the chair where the condemned is restrained. The resulting chemical reaction releases cyanide gas which kills the inmate by hypoxia. The condemned are advised to take several deep breaths once the gas has been released in order to induce rapid unconsciousness. It is typical for the prisoner to lose consciousness between one and three minutes after initial exposure to the gas, with death being pronounced ten to twelve minutes later. An exhaust fan is then activated in order to extract the gas from the chamber before the body is removed and sprayed down with ammonia.

This technique of execution is considered by some to be the most unpleasant for witnesses to view as the condemned will typically display violent convulsions similar to those of an epileptic seizure and excessive drooling.

In 1992 Robert Alton Harris was killed by lethal gas in San Quentin, California, USA. It took twenty minutes for him to die. Following this execution, on October 5, 1994, District Judge Marilyn Hall Patel ruled the gas chamber to be an inhumane method of punishment, and outlawed its use in the State of California. This ruling was upheld on December 5, 1995, by the Circuit Court of Appeals on the grounds that condemned prisoners will suffer extreme pain for several minutes. California abolished lethal gas as a method of execution, adapting the gas chamber at San Quentin to lethal injection.

The last use of the gas chamber to date in the USA was on March 3, 1999 when Walter LaGrand was executed in Arizona. The US states of Missouri and Wyoming retain the gas chamber as a method of execution, with lethal injection as an alternative.

THE GUILLOTINE

The guillotine is named after Dr. Joseph Ignace Guillotin, a Deputy of Paris. Guillotin was a humanitarian physician and member of a political reform movement which campaigned for the abolition of the death penalty. He did not invent the guillotine, but campaigned for its use as a humane alternative to execution by hanging, with the eventual aim of moving towards a complete ban on the death penalty in France. He proposed beheading on the understanding that it was instantaneous. Historically, beheading was a method of execution reserved for the social elite, because it was seen to be a noble and relatively pain-free way to die. Many executions in France involved a period of public torture before death. Burning, hanging, drawing and quartering were common practice at the time.

On October 10, 1789, (the first year of the French Revolution) during the second day of general debate on the French Penal Code, Guillotin submitted six proposals to the assembly, the second of which recommended decapitation as the sole method of criminal execution in France. He proposed that a simple machine should be built for all beheadings, and that torture be removed from the execution process. The job of designing the guillotine subsequently went to the German engineer, Tobias Schmidt, who built a device based on a design by Doctor Antoine Louis, the then Secretary of the Academy of Surgery in France. The aim of the guillotine was to execute any condemned person, without regard to their age, sex or social status.

Nicolas-Jacques Pelletier, a highwayman, was the first person to be executed by guillotine on April 25, 1792. In 1870, assistant executioner and carpenter Leon Berger incorporated a number of significant improvements into the guillotine. It was last used on September 10, 1977, on Hamida Djandoubi, a Tunisian immigrant to France. The Djandoubi execution took place at Baumettes Prison in Marseilles and was the last state execution to occur in the original European Union of countries.

The heads of decapitated people cannot speak as the larynx has been detached. They remain conscious for between thirteen to thirty seconds due to the amount of blood and oxygen available to them.

LETHAL INJECTION

In 1977, Jay Chapman, State Medical Examiner for Oklahoma, proposed lethal injection as a method for executing condemned prisoners in the USA. Subsequently, thirty-five states plus the US Military and the US Government have adopted lethal injection as a method of execution. It was first used on December 2, 1982 in Huntsville, Texas, USA to execute Charles Brooks Jr.

The procedure begins when the condemned prisoner is strapped onto a gurney. A technician then inserts an intravenous cannulae into each of the prisoner's arms after first swabbing them with alcohol. One is used for the injection of lethal drugs, and the other acts as a back-up. The tubes lead to a second room next to the execution chamber where the executioner sits.

Curtains open onto a room where the witnesses are seated. Once the needles have been inserted, the condemned is offered the chance to make a final statement before the Warden gives the signal to allow the execution to begin. The final statement allows the condemned the chance to make an apology which in turn acts to confirm his or her guilt to those assembled to witness or carry out the execution.

The first drug to be administered by lethal injection is between 2,500 to 5,000 milligrams of sodium thiopental which renders the condemned unconscious, usually within thirty seconds. This quantity of sodium thiopental is between five to ten times the recommended maximum dose for a human and has the capacity to induce death by causing the brain's electrical activity to stop completely, leading to respiratory arrest and circulatory collapse. Pancuronium bromide is then injected into the prisoner one minute later. Pancuronium bromide is a muscle relaxant which paralyzes the diaphragm and lungs to prevent breathing. This takes between one to three minutes. A final injection of potassium chloride is then administered to stop the heart beating.

Death by lethal injection typically occurs between five and twenty minutes after the order to execute has been given.

STONING

Stoning, has been used as a means of executing the condemned for thousands of years and is mentioned in the Bible.

Execution by stoning for offences which include adultery is still enshrined in the Islamic Penal Code of the Islamic Republic of Iran. Adultery, under article 74, can be proven by the witness testimony of either four just men, or three just men and two just women. A person can also confess against themselves and must present themselves before a judge four times in order for sentence to be passed. Article 77 states that witness testimony must be clear, without ambiguity and based on observation. The Penal Code also states that falsely accusing a person of adultery is a crime in itself and carries its own punishment.

It is possible for the punishment of stoning for adultery to be annulled if the adulterer repents prior to the witness testimony.

The penal code requires that for the sentence to be carried out, men must be buried in a ditch up to the waist, and women shall be buried up to the chest. If the condemned prisoner manages to escape the ditch, they will not have to face sentence again if they were convicted by means of their own confession.

The size of the stones to be thrown is prescribed in article 104 as 'not to be too large to kill the convict by one or two throws and at the same time shall not be too small to be called a stone'. The first to throw the stones are the witnesses followed by the Shari'a judge and then any others present. It is a requirement that a group of at least three believers be present when the sentence is carried out.

In December 2002, Iranian Head of Judiciary, Ayatollah Mahmoud Hashemi Shahroudi, imposed a moratorium on stoning. The suspension was successful until July 5, 2007, when Jafar Kiani, 43, who had previously been convicted of adultery, was confirmed by the Iranian judiciary to have been stoned to death in Aghche-kand, a small village near Takistan in the Northern Province of Qazvin.

TRAP DOOR GALLOWS

Hanging was abolished in the United Kingdom in 1967. The last executions to take place in England were carried out simultaneously at 8:00am on August 13, 1964. Peter Anthony Allen was hanged at Walton Prison in Liverpool, England by Robert Leslie Stewart, and Gwynne Owen Evans was hanged at Strangeways Prison in Manchester by Harry Bertrum Allen. The simultaneous hangings meant no one person was able to claim the title of the United Kingdom's last executioner.

During the twentieth century, hanging in the UK worked according to an official table of variable drops. The length the condemned dropped from the gallows and through the trap doors varied between 5' 00'' and 8' 6'' depending on the age, height, weight and strength of the prisoner. A hood was placed over the inmate's head and a noose then placed around their neck with the knot placed under the left jaw. This enabled the rope to locate itself under the chin of the prisoner on the drop, throwing the head back and breaking the spinal cord between the second and third cervical vertebrae. This results in a near instant death. If the knot is placed under the right of the chin then the head is thrown forward by the movement of the rope to the back of the head, resulting in death by strangulation. When a slipknot is used death also occurs by strangulation and takes between fifteen to twenty minutes.

A miscalculation in the distance a prisoner should drop when hanged can result in the condemned being decapitated. The last instance of this occurring in England was at Norwich Castle on November 30, 1885 on the prisoner Robert Goodale. A decapitation by miscalculation of the drop length also occurred on January 15, 2007, in Baghdad, when Barzan Ibrahim al-Tikriti (half-brother of Saddam Hussein) was given an eight foot drop.

Hanging is still used in two of the US States, New Hampshire and Washington. Washington is the only State left which has hanging as its primary method of execution. Three people have been hanged in the USA since 1976, the last being Billy Bailey in Delaware on January 25, 1996. The Walla Walla Gallows in Washington State were last used on May 27, 1994.

EYEWITNESS ACCOUNTS

ELECTRIC CHAIR

An eyewitness recorded this account of the execution of William Kemmler (the first man to be put to death by electric chair). It was published in the New York Times on August 7, 1890.

'Warden Durston had gone to the cell of the condemned man. He carried with him the death warrant, and he read it to Kemmler as the latter sat on the side of his bunk. Kemmler's sole remark when the Warden had finished was: "All right, I am ready." The Warden then left the cell, and in the entrance hall above met the witnesses who had accepted his invitation. While most of the visitors loitered about the hall, Warden Durston went with J. C. Veiling, Kemmler's old Buffalo keeper, to the murderer's cell. Kemmler was apparently greatly pleased to see Veiling, and insisted that he should remain to breakfast with him. To this position Veiling assented, and a good breakfast was soon set before them. While they were waiting for it the Rev. Drs. Houghton and Yates entered the cage. Kemmler greeted them in a pleasant manner, and they talked with him for a few minutes on the subject of his coming death. Then the clergymen and Kemmler knelt upon the floor, the murderer in his shirt sleeves, and a prayer for the soul of the condemned man was offered up.

Breakfast followed, and throughout the meal Kemmler was in the best of spirits. After the meal Kemmler was asked if he had any objection to having his hair cut, and he said he had not. Veiling therefore produced a pair of shears and cut the hair of the murderer's head. Kemmler sat smiling while the shears were being plied. Veiling was very nervous, and made a sorry job of the haircutting. When he had finished his work the crown of Kemmler's head from which the hair had been cut had the appearance of a great scar.

Several times the murderer addressed Veiling. "They say I am afraid to die," he said, "but they will find that I a'int. I want you to stay right by me, Joe, and see me through this thing and I will promise you that I won't make any trouble."

The last moment in the old cage came soon and Kemmler arose to follow the Warden into the adjoining room. He had previously bidden the faithful Daniel farewell. His eyes roved over the dingy quarters a moment and then he looked straight toward the door. "Come William," said the Warden, and together they walked into the chamber of death. A solemn hush had fallen upon the witnesses as Warden Durston left the death chamber to bring in the doomed man. There was a very apparent nervousness among the men, used as most of them were to sights that would chill ordinary men's blood. The uncertainty of what was to come filled them with awe. Somebody attempted to speak, but his voice was lost in its own faintness. A step was heard outside. All eyes turned toward the door leading into the chamber. Warden Durston appeared, and beside him was the man who stood on the verge of an awful death. Yet there was nothing in his appearance to suggest this. His face was composed and he walked in an easy manner as though he were entering a room to receive a party of friends.

After he had crossed the threshold there was an instance of the deadest silence. It was broken by Warden Durston.

"Gentlemen," he said, "this is William Kemmler." And Kemmler bowed.

"Gentlemen," he said, "I wish you all good luck. I believe I am going to a good place, and I am ready to go. I want only to say that a great deal has been said about me that is untrue. I am bad enough. It is cruel to make me out worse."

As he finished this little speech, he bowed again, and was about to sit down in a chair which had been placed beside the death chair. Warden Durston, seeing this, stepped forward, and Kemmler, noticing his action, saw that the time had come, and instead of sitting where he had intended, turned and easily dropped into the seat. Still he did it much as one might after a long walk fall into the welcome arms of an easy chair. He sat with the light from the window streaming full on his face, and immediately in front of him was the semicircle of witnesses. Warden Durston stepped to the chair, and at his request Kemmler arose. It was desired to see whether his clothing had been cut away at the base of the spine so as to allow a clean contact between the electrode and the flesh. It was found that the outer garments had been cut, but the lower clothing had not been. Durston took out a pocket knife and cut two small triangular pieces out of the shirt.

Then Kemmler easily settled back into the chair again. As he did so Durston started to get the rear piece in position. A murmur of surprise passed among the witnesses when Kemmler turned calmly to the Warden and in such tones as one might speak to a barber who was shaving him, said calmly: "Now take your time and do it all right, Warden. There is no rush. I don't want to take any chances on this thing, you know."

"All right, William," answered Durston, and then began to adjust the headpiece. It looked horrible with its leather bands crossing the doomed man's forehead and chin and partially concealing his features. When the job was finished Durston stepped back. Kemmler shook his head as one might when trying on a new hat, and then just as coolly as before he said: "Warden, just make it a little tighter. We want everything all right, you know."

The Warden did as requested and then started to fix the straps around the body, arms, and legs. There were eleven of them. As each was buckled Kemmler would put some strain on it so as to see if it were tight enough. All appeared to suit him, and in answer to a question by the Warden he answered: "All right." Durston then stepped to the door. The last minute had come.

Standing on the threshold he turned and said quietly: "Is it all ready?" Nobody spoke. Kemmler merely lifted his eyes for a moment and turned them enough to catch a glimpse of the bright, warm sunlight that was streaming through the window of the death chamber.

"Good-bye, William," said Durston, and a click was heard. The "Good-bye" was the signal to the men at the lever. The great experiment of electrical execution had been launched. New-York State had thrown off forever the barbarities, the inhumanities of hanging its criminals. But had it? Words will not keep pace with what followed. Simultaneously with the click of the lever the body of the man in the chair straightened. Every muscle of it seemed to be drawn to its highest tension. It seemed as though it might have been thrown across the chamber were it not for the straps which held it. There was no movement of the eyes. The body was as rigid as though cast bronze, save for the index finger of the right hand, which closed up so tightly that the nail penetrated the flesh on the first joint, and the blood trickled out on the arm of the chair. Drs. Spitzka and Macdonald stood in front of the dead or dying man. Beside them was Dr. Daniels, holding a stop-watch.

After the first convulsion there was not the slightest movement of Kemmler's body. An ashen pallor had overspread his features. What physicians know as the "death spots" appeared on his skin. Five seconds passed, ten seconds, fifteen seconds, sixteen and seventeen. It was just 6:43 o'clock. Dr. Spitzka, shaking his head, said: "He is dead." Warden Durston pressed the signal button, and at once the dynamo was stopped. The assembled witnesses who had sat as still as mutes up to this point gave breath to a sigh. The great strain was over. Then the eyes that had been momentarily turned from Kemmler's body returned to it and gazed with horror on what they saw. The men rose from their chairs impulsively and groaned at the agony they felt. "Great God! he is alive!" some one said; "Turn on the current," said another; "See, he breathes," said a third; "For God's sake kill him and have it over," said a representative of one of the press associations, and then, unable to bear the strain, he fell on the floor in a dead faint. District Attorney Quimby groaned audibly and rushed from the room.

Drs. Spitzka and Macdonald stepped toward the chair. Warden Durston, who had started to loosen the electrode on the head, raised it slightly and then hastily screwed it back into place. Kemmler's body had become limp and settled down in the chair. His chest was raising and falling and there was a heavy breathing that was perceptible to all. Kemmler was, of course, entirely unconscious. Drs. Spitzka and Macdonald kept their wits about them. Hastily they examined the man, not touching him, however. Turning to Warden Durston, who had just finished getting the head electrode back in place, Dr. Spitzka said: "Have the current turned on again, quick – no delay." Durston sprang to the door, and in an instant had sounded the two bells, which informed the man at the lever that the current must be turned on.

Again came the click as before, and again the body of the unconscious wretch in the chair became rigid as one of bronze. It was awful, and the witnesses were so horrified by the ghastly sight that they could not take their eyes off it. The dynamo did not seem to run smoothly. The current could be heard sharply snapping. Blood began to appear on the face of the wretch in the chair. It stood on the face like sweat. The capillary or small blood vessels under the skin were being ruptured. But there was worse than that. An awful odour began to permeate the death chamber, and then, as though to cap the climax of this fearful sight, it was seen that the hair under and around the electrode on the head and the flesh at the base of the spine was singeing. The stench was unbearable.

How long this second execution lasted – for it was a second execution, if there was any real life in the body when the current was turned on for the second time – is not really known by anybody. Those who held watches were too much horrified to follow them. Some said afterward that it had lasted a minute; one said it lasted fully four minutes and a half. Opinions ranged all the way between these figures. Dr. Spitzka, who was as cool as any man could be under such circumstances, says it was not more than a minute. It was 6:51 o'clock when the signal went to the man at the lever to shut off the current. Kemmler had been in the chair just eight minutes from the time the current was first turned on. There is nobody among the witnesses present who can tell just how much of that time the current was passing through the body of Kemmler.

As soon as the current was off again Warden Durston rapidly unscrewed the electrodes and unbuckled the straps. Kemmler's body again was limp. This time he was surely dead. There was no doubt of that. The body was left sitting upright in the chair and the witnesses of the tragedy that had been enacted passed out into the stone corridors as miserable, as weak-kneed a lot of men as can be imagined. It had nauseated all but a few of them, and the sick ones had to be looked out for. They were all practically silent for some time. Their minds were too busy to enable them to talk. They all seemed to act as though they felt that they had taken part in a scene that would be told to the world as a public shame, as a legal crime.'

FIRING SQUAD

John Albert Taylor was the last person to be executed by firing squad in the USA to date. This happened in Utah on January 26, 1996 at 12:03 am. Paul Murphy (from KTVX Channel 4, Salt Lake City) said:

'We saw this very large man strapped to a chair. His eyes were darting back and forth. He was strapped to the chair by his hands and feet and lifted his chin for Warden Hank Geletka to secure a strap around his neck and place the black hood over his head. At 12:03 a.m., on the count of three, the five riflemen standing 23 feet away fired at a white cloth target pinned over Taylor's heart. Blood darkened the chest area of his navy blue clothing, and four minutes later, a doctor pronounced him dead. Very little blood spilled into the pan under the chair's mesh seat. As the volley hit him, Taylor's hands squeezed up, went down, and came up and squeezed again. His chest was covered in blood.'

GUILLOTINE

A number of French doctors have looked into the time severed heads remained conscious. Dr. Jacques Beaurieux carried out an experiment on the head of Henri Languille, a prisoner who was executed on June 28, 1905 at 5:30am. He wrote:

'The head fell on the severed surface of the neck and I did not therefore have to take it up in my hands. I was not obliged even to touch it in order to set it upright. Chance served me well for the observation, which I wished to make. Here, then, is what I was able to note immediately after the decapitation: the eyelids and lips of the guillotined man worked in irregularly rhythmic contractions for about five or six seconds. This phenomenon has been remarked by all those finding themselves in the same conditions as myself for observing what happens after the severing of the neck...

I waited for several seconds. The spasmodic movements ceased. The face relaxed, the lids half closed on the eyeballs, leaving only the white of the conjunctiva visible, exactly as in the dying whom we have occasion to see every day in the exercise of our profession, or as in those just dead. It was then that I called in a strong, sharp voice: "Languille!" I saw the eyelids slowly lift up, without any spasmodic contractions – I insist advisedly on this peculiarity – but with an even movement, quite distinct and normal, such as happens in everyday life, with people awakened or torn from their thoughts. Next Languille's eyes very definitely fixed themselves on mine and the pupils focused themselves. I was not, then, dealing with the sort of vague dull look without any expression, that can be observed any day in dying people to whom one speaks: I was dealing with undeniably living eyes which were looking at me. After several seconds, the eyelids closed again, slowly and evenly, and the head took on the same appearance as it had had before I called out.

It was at that point that I called out again and, once more, without any spasm, slowly, the eyelids lifted and undeniably living eyes fixed themselves on mine with perhaps even more penetration than the first time. Then there was a further closing of the eyelids, but now less complete. I attempted the effect of a third call; there was no further movement – and the eyes took on the glazed look which they have in the dead.'

81

HANGING

According to an article in the Iranian newspaper Kayhan, a man named Niaz Ali survived a hanging in February 1996.

Niaz Ali, who was believed to be in his thirties at the time, was condemned for killing a man near the city of Hamadan three years earlier. He reportedly stayed suspended on the rope for twenty minutes before being pronounced dead, after which he was taken to a morgue. On arriving to claim the body, his brother found Niaz Ali's heart was beating slowly.

Niaz Ali, once conscious, was returned to jail. While there he described the experience of being hanged to a reporter from Kayhan:

'That first second lasted like a thousand years.... I felt my arms and legs jerking out of control... Up on the gallows in the dark I was trying to fill my lungs with air but they were crumpled like plastic bags.'

Source: Amnesty International

STONING

This account of a stoning which occurred in the late 1990's was described in July 2006 by a former prisoner and fellow inmate of a woman known as Zahra. It was published by Amnesty International in January 2008, in the report, 'Iran, End Executions by Stoning'.

She said that she had been befriended by Zahra, a round-faced woman with dark eyes and short hair, in the run-up to Zahra's trial. She reported that after Zahra returned from court, she was exhausted by the flogging she had received but relieved because she had been told she would be released the next day. The prisoners celebrated. The next day, however, Zahra was executed:

'When Zahra was led out of our quarters, with all her hopes and dreams of being released, she was directed to a solitary confinement where her stoning sentence would be carried out. It was there that she realized what was about to take place. There, she was given an Islamic atonement ritual and after reading some words of the Qur'an she was placed in a special ditch with only her head and neck sticking out.

In the corner of the room they had piled up some stones... In the middle of this act, Zahra had struggled her way out of the ditch but the observing judge had ordered the guards to return her to the ditch. All this time, her deaf son Javad had been witnessing the act.

At the end, a man named Taghi, using a cement block, struck the last blow. And then it was all over...

Zahra left us with many untold words but her memory as a woman, a human being and a mother will remain with all of us. We all make mistakes in our lives, and although she had committed an immoral act, such punishment in my opinion, and most others, is barbaric and should be abolished.'

Source: Meydaan

CONCLUSION

CONCLUSION
Nigel Rodley

In September 1973 the International Council of Amnesty International, representing all its sections around the world, adopted a resolution making it a totally abolitionist organization. Previously the organisation had restricted itself to calling for abolition in political cases; now it was abolitionist regardless of the nature of the offence.

That was my first year as Amnesty International's first legal officer and the Swedish section had asked me to draft the resolution, a welcome task, as I had been an abolitionist since I read a newspaper account of the gassing of Caryl Chessman in 1960. I had at that time no expectation that I would live to see the day of universal abolition. In 1973 only about twenty-five countries were abolitionist, and this was 211 years after the Italian philosopher Cesare di Beccaria had first exposed the moral and utilitarian bankruptcy of the death penalty as a tool of criminal policy; at such a rate of progress the goal of abolition would not be achieved for centuries.

Less than four decades on, 102 States − nearly four times the 1973 figure and constituting a majority of the world's States − are now abolitionist in law for all ordinary crimes. A further thirty-six States are considered abolitionist de facto, not having executed anyone for the past ten years. So, 138 out of 197 States may be deemed abolitionist. It is likely that Amnesty International's campaigning played a substantial role in this evolution.

If we look at the world by region, we find that with Russia maintaining a formal moratorium on the death penalty (the reversal of which would represent a cataclysmic breakdown in the structure of the new Europe from the Atlantic to the Urals) 850 million people in that region are no longer under the shadow of the death penalty. Latin America, which pioneered abolition in the 19th Century, is now overwhelmingly abolitionist. Even in Africa, which in 1973 had the death penalty in all but the four Portuguese colonies, - abolition is steadily moving north from the Cape to the Sahara. Add de facto abolition in Algeria and the movement has reached the southern Mediterranean. Moreover, Asia, which is responsible for a large majority of the world's executions (some three quarters of the total for 2008), can boast some thirteen States that are abolitionist in law or practice. Of course, despite this worldwide spread of abolition, one cannot ignore the fact that fifty-nine countries, some of considerable size and influence, are retentionist in practice, notably, China, India and the United States.

Disappointing as it may be, it is not surprising that international law has not been able to proscribe the death penalty. At first sight it might be thought that, since international law enshrines respect for the right to life high in its pantheon of firmly established human rights rules, the death penalty would be seen as an obvious violation of that right. Similarly, the layperson could be forgiven for assuming that the international legal prohibition of torture and cruel, inhuman or degrading treatment or punishment would rule out the death penalty – particularly since it is generally accepted that corporal punishment does fall foul of the prohibition.

Unfortunately, however, logic is not necessarily the determinant of law and international law is no exception. On the contrary, it is a system of law that is heavily influenced by the practice of States. This is because it is a system of law made by States for States, each of which is as sovereign and equal as every other one. This means it is not a 'majority rules' system, but one based significantly on State consent. So, generally rules of international law have to be interpreted in the light of what States actually do or claim the right to do, and as long as so many and such significant States continue to defend their right to retain the death penalty, international law is incapable of declaring the practice illegal.

Indeed, the position is not helped by the fact that the right-to-life provisions of several human rights treaties, including the International Covenant on Civil and Political Rights (which has been accepted by 162 States from all parts of the world), also have language allowing for the use of the death penalty provided that it respects certain basic criteria. These criteria are significant: the penalty must be imposed only for the most serious crimes committed by persons over eighteen, and only after a fair trial with a right of appeal and the possibility of obtaining clemency. Another criterion is that the penalty must involve the least possible suffering, a notion that imposes on human rights bodies the conceptually impossible task of choosing among options none of which can be humane.

Just as it is not possible to interpret the right to life as excluding the death penalty, the problem cannot be circumvented by simply arguing the penalty is (like corporal punishment) a form of prohibited cruel, inhuman or degrading punishment. After all, that notion too has to be construed in the light of retentionist State practice.

Nevertheless, the political and legal momentum is unmistakably abolitionist. In addition to the actual trend of individual States to abandon the penalty, the United Nations General Assembly has since 1971 adopted resolutions referring to the 'desirability' of abolishing the death penalty. In the 1980s and 1990s a body of resistance to this policy built up, successfully blocking further developments, but by 2007 the Assembly was able to adopt a resolution reaffirming the position and calling for a moratorium on the use of the death penalty, albeit with a substantial number of dissenters.

In addition, abolitionist treaty documents have been adopted in the form of protocols to regional and international human rights treaties. It is true that only seventy-one States have accepted the Second Optional Protocol to the International Covenant on Civil and Political Rights, which aims at the abolition of the death penalty. Of course, only abolitionist countries can be expected to become parties to the Protocol and it is understandable that a number of such countries simply do not see the formalities of adherence to be a political priority. But the essential point is that the protocols are there as strong evidence that the death penalty is not just a matter of any State's internal criminal policy, it is also, unavoidably a human rights issue.

Professor Sir Nigel Rodley is the Chair of the Human Rights Centre at the University of Essex, a member of the United Nations Human Rights Committee and a Commissioner of the International Commission of Jurists.

NO HUMAN WAY TO KILL

AFTERWORD
Robert Priseman

An execution is the planned killing of a human being. It requires several people to do something, and yet, no one person needs to accept a direct responsibility. The act of execution appears to involve a process of ritualisation which devolves responsibility away from the individual. It is the final result of an often drawn out chain of events which begins with a crime, moves on to a trial and sometimes an appeals process. It may involve the manufacture of specialist equipment and will usually involve the drawing up of special protocols.

Executions culminate with a concentration of individuals who all participate, either directly or indirectly, whether as a medic, reporter, member of a tie-down team or Warden, all of whom are able to claim no direct culpability for the event at hand. I came to wonder while working on this book, whether executions would take place at all if they were never reported, if the equipment used was never sold or if a spiritual advisor was not at hand for the condemned. The unused passive alternative is to lock someone away and deny them food and water, which will end a person's life within a couple of weeks.

The ritual of execution takes on many forms which are often peculiar to a specific country, such as the guillotine in France, the garrotte in Spain and the single person gas chamber in the USA. Concern for the physical well being of the condemned is expressed through the desire to end their life as quickly and painlessly as possible. It is witnessed through the provision of a mattress on the gurney and padding for the seat of the electric chair, a concern which seems to suggest a disquiet felt by those taking part. I would argue that this disquiet is caused by the process of turning a taboo in to a legally sanctioned act.

By devolving responsibility, no one person can be held accountable for breaking what is an otherwise strict moral and social code against killing within society. Killing only becomes acceptable when it is carried out in someone else's name. That name may be the name of God, of society or even of the family, but it is never in the name of an individual.

93

The plates were etched by Robert Priseman in 2007 and editioned by Jan and Ian Wilkinson at the Goldmark Atelier, Uppingham, Rutland, United Kingdom in 2008. The etchings are published and are available via www.goldmarkart.com.

This book has been made possible with the help and support of the following organisations:

Amicus, Amnesty International, European Commission, Goldmark Gallery, Liberty, Murder Victims' Families for Reconciliation, Penal Reform International, Reprieve, The Human Rights Centre of the University of Essex, World Coalition Against the Death Penalty.

www.artfractures.com

Made in the USA
Lexington, KY
10 November 2012